EARLY PRAISE FOR

OPEN PASSAGES

"These poetic passages feel like blessings, prayer, the quiet voice of the heart. They acknowledge the beauty of peace within the soul and the courage it takes to protect that sacred inner space amidst the complex world of daily life. This is one of those books worth keeping by the bedside to read a page on rising or at the close of day, inviting us to return to who we are."

—IVAN M. GRANGER, Founder of *Poetry Chaikhana*, Editor of *The Longing in Between: Sacred Poetry from Around the World*

"This book is full of simple but profound life lessons that read like poetry from the world's greatest mystics- free of dogma and throbbing with emotion. Self-knowledge is a messy ride, but Susan herself is a compassionate, eloquent guide through the bright spots and shadows, the ecstatic moments and the quiet, solitary ones- reminding us that, no matter what, we always have what we need to navigate all of it. Susan covers all the "major" topics: change, death, closure, heartbreak, purpose, and the seasons and cycles of one's personal journey. She compels the reader to ask the age-old questions: Who am I? What is my true power? How do I deal with pain and loss? What does it mean to connect with the divine? How can we "find" ourselves in a world where death and change are the only constants? All the same, the passages in this book inspire hope rather than despair. Susan shows us how dancing with both our gifts and our wounds, and welcoming everything that comes our way with curiosity and openness, is the key to our authenticity. Full of passionate honesty and feeling, Open Passages is a gift to all the dreamers and sensitive souls out there. I love opening this book at random and being led to whatever message I need to read that day. It's like opening a present- and that present is ME."

—KELLY MCNELIS, Author, Founder of
Women For One Movement

"An exquisite and most beautifully written book. This book is to be read many times as one would feast on delicious food. A powerful call to know and value who we are. A poignant invitation to the nobility of authenticity, humanity and love."

—CHRIS SAADE, Author of *Evolutionary Love Relationships* and *Second Wave Spirituality*

"Susan's voice is as evocative as Sappho's harp. She muses about the journey of the mutual strings of the heart, and the ancient quest for the enlightened spirit to live authentically in the light of truth. Behold, she pens - breaths 'words which I command are immortal'."

—CLARA MACRI, Writer/Contributor (Huffington Post),
Philanthropist, Broker for the Arts

"So much in life is hasty. If you take the time to read Susan Frybort's Passages, you will begin to look inward, pondering the direction of your life. Not in a guilt-ridden way, but with possibility and hope. Her short, poetic passages, will affirm the strength that exists within yourself. I felt whispers of encouragement, empathy in my trials, and a determination to be free."

—DAVID SANDUM, Artist, Award-Winning Author of
*I'll Run Till the Sun Goes Down: A Memoir
about Depression and Discovering Art*

"Susan Frybort carries the profound ability of revealing the sacred in the most unsure moments and enlightening the heart to find the holy when all seems ordinary. Through these Passages a courageous love calls to be remembered and Susan's words remind us of what has been hidden right here all along in the most precious expressions of human life."

—JAYANANDA, Author of *Living with
Love & Light of Heart*

"Susan has deep-dived into an inner narrative. At all the deepest, most profound moments that journey touches everything – the inner, the outer and all between. It is more than a narrative. It is personal, it is universal, it is cosmic, it is very much woven of the stuff of being on earth. It reflects the deepest skills of a weaver, a receiver, a soul on the road. I am no reviewer of books, I am no experienced assessor of a narrative reflection of the trials and tribulations of existence, but I trust my instincts and my heart to register authentic love and soul when I encounter it. Susan has created and is sharing here a gigantic, soft, tender, powerful series of moments of love and soul energy. I know Susan knows her stuff and she has lived and breathed the weave of life the way a season always tries to be a season to the benefit of all of life, all seasons. Susan is the spirit who embraces spirit – she is the soul who clothes herself in soul and she is a fine writer, an exceptional narrative artist. Be it a skirt, a poem, be it a story or a painting, be it a photograph or an artistic expression that refuses any category – Susan lives there, breathes there and loves there with every fiber of her soul. Open Passages extolls the absolute and unadulterated value of openness. I am a stupid person but I do try and I do come from the hope that trying to be open and trying to share soul and spirit, and trying to be practical and down to earth can give each of my fellow human-beings a sense of hope and value and love. Susan is love and reading all her words was bathing in love and generosity. Thank you Susan for taking this journey."

—DEAN PASCH, Artist, Poet & Filmmaker

OPEN
PASSAGES

Doors and Windows to the Soul

SUSAN FRYBORT

ENREALMENT PRESS
TORONTO, CANADA

Published by Enrealment Press
PO Box 64
Acton, Ontario
Canada L7J 2M2

Cover photo by © Jodielee I Dreamstime.com
Front Cover Embellishment by Romanova Ekaterina/Shutterstock
Author photos by Lindsay Knapp
Cover design by Susan Frybort. Book design by Allyson Woodrooffe

Printed in the USA

Library and Archives Canada Cataloguing in Publication

Frybort, Susan, 1966-, author
    Open passages : doors and windows to the soul / Susan Frybort.

Poems.
Issued in print and electronic formats.
ISBN 978-0-9947843-7-7 (softcover)
ISBN 978-0-9947843-8-4 (PDF)

    I. Title.

PS3606.R93O64 2017   811'.6   C2017-900950-8
                                         C2017-900951-6

Dedicated to you.
As you open this book
and walk through its passages,
may its encouraging words
forever remain in your heart.

Dear Reader,

Welcome to *Open Passages: Doors and Windows to the Soul.*

Many go through life being tormented by negative emotions, not clearly able to reference why or how to understand and overcome them. Feeling unseen, longing to be heard, a deep sense of unworthiness and craving recognition have stifled opportunities to experience joy and growth. As we live in our modern society, what we can hear under its ever-increasing pulse are the outpourings of not feeling good enough, regret for what has happened in life, feeling left behind, perceptions of inadequacy and being undervalued as a deserving human being. The fallout from trauma and circumstance ends up being additional tonnage encumbering praiseworthy spirits and preventing them from soaring to wondrous heights. My concern for the human condition grows deeper the further I delve into heart matters and what it means to feel alive and relevant, what it means to hold faith and passion dearly, and what it means to understand the most subterranean fears and anxieties. Just like each divine soul over time, I have had my share of heartbreak and trauma, to which I express in this book. For years, my written entries have remained private, my journaling during specific times of distress or challenge, or while transitioning from one place to another, was both a solace and offered restoration. Within these pages, I unveil the windows of my inner world, my intimate reflections, and my personal perceptions as prose written in passages. I share my ineffable bliss and undeniable sorrow. I offer my eager inquiries along with my best conclusions. My desire is to render healing to the collective wound by opening the entries and walkways that have and continue to lead me towards my own wholeness. My intent is that you identify with at least one validating entry or poem, then find the courage to open the door connecting you to your next destination in life. And my wish is, after reading from these encouraging meditations, they will have awakened in you a new sense of hope.

Read from these Open Passages for affirmation and gain the strength to step through the imminent portal that will guide you fully into the light... where you can see how much you are appreciated, accept you are truly worthy, and feel you are loved, unabashedly and powerfully.

With love and gratitude,
Susan Frybort

OPEN PASSAGES

Doors and Windows to the Soul

SUSAN FRYBORT

Life is not passing you by. Life is inviting you in. Inviting you into the simple and sudden moments of quiet, yet invigorating bliss that veer on the wind and into your stilled body, sending tingles through your spirit. Life is not passing you by. Life is drawing you close. Pulling you in and calling you towards an awakening spark that will ignite the purest of imaginative thought and vision into being. Life is not overlooking you, underestimating you, or merely passing through. Life is subtly requesting you take all you've held safely within and give it room to be birthed into creative expression. No, life has not heartlessly given up on you. Life is graciously standing by.

LIGHT THE WAY FOR LOVE

They say beauty comes from a spirit that has weathered many hardships in life and somehow continues with resilience. Grace can be found in a soul who ages softly, even amid the tempest.

I think the loveliest by far is the one whose gentle heart bears a hundred scars from caring, yet still finds a way to pick up the lamp, one more time, to light the way for love.

Why look for an outward sign—
on the gust of the wind,
after a flash of bold lightning,
or by probing the deep and
mystical language of the universe—
when the greatest indicators
are already within you?

Under the skin of reason
and past the layers of logic
rests the wise perceptive
bones of your intuition.

Inside the rich body of reflections
weaving clues throughout
your sleeping dreams.

Within the shy flutters and
faint waves of feeling sweeping
through your being,
coaxing you to trust,
urging you to listen, all saying:

Come, retreat to the woods of your own
knowing and follow your inner stream.

It takes a powerful person to cry out despite those who'd prefer the convenience of silence. It takes a fearless person to allow their sadness to come out from the tight box of cultural expectations to be expressed and processed. And it takes a world of strength for that same person to be true to their feelings, own their emotional territory—to walk into the very chaos of its outright messiness—and uncover the paragons of victory and joy that were held by them, for such an aching long time, so quietly within.

THE GRATITUDE IN CLOSURE

If you are human, you'll discover in life that there are certain events which become suspended in your mind, unsecured and unsettled. While you thought you had progressed, you may not genuinely feel the clear and definite energy around a past relationship or circumstance to suggest an authentic conclusion. The loose ends have not been woven back in any way that makes sense. It does not feel as simple as *just letting go*. You want to feel recognition, acceptance, and understanding—for yourself and the experience—so it can all be knit together and enable you to grow forth. If and once those final stitches have been sewn to join the remaining pieces, you will feel a new gratitude when coming full circle. Closure is what makes it feel clearer. Closure is what takes you onward with positivity. Though it is not always possible, may you find this blessed completion however and wherever it is so needed. It will allow you to move forward in peace and move gratefully on.

To reveal the hidden parts of you, however raw, from the private corners of your heart and out into the open takes guts. To allow your ravenous spirit to become uninhibited and soar takes certain bravery.

Love is here for you and has a courage all its own. And you can let the power of what you love guide you to that freedom.

For one day soon you will step into your own stunning universe—beyond the myths, outside any limitations or predictions, far from the illusions this life invents—as you answer the call to uncover the many starlit truths contained inside your incomparable soul. You will be reborn to fresh and glorious revelations only you can carry to completion. And while all the infinite possibilities expand within, may you sing aloud, rejoicing in your new birth, no longer owned by anyone's idea of who you should be.

You're afraid of changing.
Change tenderly calls for you to open
the places within that have been guarded
with a warrior's vigilance for decades.

Change beckons you to come forward and
view the inner landscapes that have been
shrouded in mystery for years.

Change won't offer you promises or
guarantees. But, as the rest of the world
moves along, the pages turn and others go
forth all around, change whispers,
I am still here and I have not forgotten you.

It is not too late to embrace change.

Empyreal Calling

You don't have to wait to be accepted by a spiritual tribe to experience the deep nurturing love wants to offer. You don't have to invest your mind in one specific outcome to win. You don't have to prove worthiness to become a chosen one.

When you are ready, you can step into the majesty of your empyreal calling, which is to become your truest self in this marvel of a world.

What has happened has already happened. There is no going back. Although you can't travel in reverse to pinpoint the exact beginning and do it all differently, you are neither bound to walk the same old beaten tracks. And you don't have to exhaust yourself in the efforts of making a painful comeback. You don't need to search frantically for just the right setting to emerge anew. For there is an opening that separates you from *what was* and *what will be*. It is an offering given to you by each present moment, called *now*. Now is when and where the inception of your authentic awakening can begin. Now is where your confused and frightened self can rise to walk with measured strides. Now is when you can take a step up higher in your thinking as you're opening to seeing your surroundings with a much clearer and deepening lens. You can do better now. Because now is the genesis of your transformation, the apex where all the truthful places in you shine brighter than ever before and continue to expand within you even more. *Starting right now.*

As you rise in your transformation, you might feel yourself being pulled back to your former placement. Remember, you don't have to remain trapped in what it is others may think of you, or lodged in the previous notions of your ideal self. You can step out and away from the decay of old beliefs which no longer hold any true meaning. Be encouraged, there is more for you, even after the last petal falls away. Enclosed and nestled within the tiniest seed waits the resplendence of what is to come. You will grow to unfold to your fullest in due season— like a blossoming rose who knows no other way.

There is no use feeling ashamed of stripping away all the skins that no longer apply. There is no disgrace in allowing the complete spectrum of emotions to come into view. The soul cannot sustain synthetic feelings. The bones hold no interest in supporting anything feigned or untrue.

Love will genuinely listen to the heart
that is honestly speaking.

When we give with love and honesty, numbers, figures, price tags and ratings fail to measure the worth of our offering. Outside approval cannot validate or determine the true merit of a kind gesture. In a culture of extreme spending and expectation, I still believe the best gifts can't be bought and are wrapped in heartfelt sincerity. And it is through the act of giving itself that we grow as human beings. You really do have a gift to give in life, and the world is simply a brighter place when you share it.

Sometimes the silent ones shed quiet tears. For those who carry the sadness of loss after weeks, months, even years have passed: Time will go forward, yet because you have loved so deeply, the sorrow you feel remains heavy. Allow the space for grief to stretch out its beauty and sing out its pain... to be cherished in remembrance as part of love's story.

The Consolation for Never

Some places are just too complicated to get to.
Some heartaches feel like mountains too high to scale.
Some people will never find the courage to approach
the shining mirror you have become.
Some wounds may never fully heal
this side of the veil.

Some plans will never turn out the way they ought to.
And the stars will never grant each childhood dream.
Some will appear to you unexpected to open wide
or block the way. For many things in life are
not always what they seem.

So, the consolation for *never* can be as simple
as the moment you behold everything you gain,
when you realize the most remarkable of treasures
is within arm's reach of you,
and as plain as the recognition
of this gifted day.

You are a blessing counting wonder. You were not sheltered by a padded life of comfort, or favored from the very start with luxury and convenience. You know what it is like to be exhausted before the fall. But somewhere along the line you never allowed yourself to become steeped in self-pity, nor did you meditate on what was always going wrong in your world. Instead, you reached for the blessings to counteract your worry and considered all that was right and true. Your love for life and its many small graces is the unexpected beauty others admire in you. And it is this trait that leads to more life within your infinite collection of blessings.

A smile can be the starting point for joy,
the beginning of a bond,
and an unexpected peacemaker.

CALLING ALL THE DREAMERS

Calling all the dreamers,
romantics and enterprising schemers…
and yes, you too, the striving novices
and aspiring achievers.
You're the ones who go back
to the drawing board
after every time you falter,
inventing brand new
inspiration before the critics
and disbelievers.
You are the stars that ascend
with bold and painstaking attempts
to bring a light that wholly shimmers,
while your faith is the stuff
that moves mountains, hearts and minds.
For long ago your quiet dreams
had little doubt you'd give them glory,
and would not grow dimmer.

You bring the world a spark of hope
as you rise and fully shine.

THE FLOW OF PURPOSE

Purpose doesn't always appear as solid and concrete. In fact, it can often resemble liquid, moving through its subtle forms as it reaches various stages. For some, getting clear can prove difficult, and searching for purpose—or one's reason for being paired with goals and intentions—can bring a sense of pressure or discouragement, as if they must recognize it immediately and make a noticeably meaningful impact. But really, purpose has been streaming through you since you were born. In little experiences, big mistakes, and everyday accomplishments. Feel the fluidity of purpose when you get off course or lose sight as it begins to pull you back into its current. Purpose is in the way you seem to glide effortlessly through tasks and how delight flows from your fingertips while you're creating. There are times when you may not be sure, and then there are times when you unmistakably know. Because once a purpose is discovered it becomes a guiding point in which the mind, body, and spirit move joyfully from.

I commit to memory your light,
to remember my way back to love.

Under the cloak of formality there is a boy of wonder and scraped knees trying to secure his place inside of life's perplexing picture. Behind the strong and smiling dress-up is a girl who is finding her way in this big, mixed-up world. We need not be adorned with disguises from day to day, or put on fearless, bold charades when we're experiencing confusion below the surface. Even while we're being grown-ups, our image needn't be donned with daring faces to cover up our childlike bewilderment while it's still okay to admit when we're afraid. Let us remain accepting of how we feel underneath as we make our way towards what is real and genuinely courageous: *The wonderment of self-discovery.*

You can see the world is quietly hurting inside when you look past its rugged demeanor. You may be asking yourself how you might be of any help, feeling your endeavors have little impact in the face of the world's most urgent needs. Where do you even begin? Begin by simply lifting your thoughts in any way you fashion and believe. Believe that you will find your offering and begin to sew one even stitch at a time. When the world feels like its unraveling and coming apart at the seams, all efforts of giving serve to mend.

Though the doors in this life swing closed all around,
let my heart remain open and available.

LET NOTHING CORRODE YOUR SOUL

Just as it is essential to cherish
your presence among the stars,
there are times and places in which
you must declare you don't belong.

You don't belong to unloving humans.
You don't belong in oppressive relationships.
You don't belong with toxic friends.
Let nothing corrode your soul.

Above everything else,
treasure your light
by honoring yourself.

In a world where rugs are pulled
and tables turned, words fall flat
and hearts get burned,
there are three things
I know for sure:

Life goes on,
love endures, and
gratitude is worry's cure.

I'm stepping out from wooded shadows and into the bright arrival of a fresh day. Beyond the forest, rugged trees give way to a clearing as I walk beside new possibilities. Along the path, I gather tattered pieces from seasons past to place with care upon the mantle. And to my surprise what I discover, resting nestled and preserved, are scattered dreams now recollected, their colors vibrantly reminding amid the slender pines. Entwined with twigs and fallen needles, I find childhood dreams that have lost their way, I uncover wild dreams yet unbroken, and dreams that used to keep me up at night, still restless and alive. Now is the time I pick them up, dust them off and let them breathe into a wider opening. Let their pulse race free with promise. Let them blend with each morning's faithful light.

THE NIGHT BEFORE CHANGE

As your dreams pace restlessly
between wake and sleep,
it is the eve of transformation.
Old identities no longer fit.
Transition calls out in the night.
You sit on the hinge
ready to swing into change,
trembling, not knowing the outcome.

Courage stands by on this threshold,
when you are ready to begin—
completely and finally.
Courage remains as you bloom into life,
then step over into a bold new reality.

On this last day of winter, under the glow of twilight in a field yet scattered with patches of softening snow, I stood reflecting in harmony with the evening's luminous hues. As I become older, I learn more and grow further. I can look within myself just as profoundly as when I gaze into a night replete with intricate cluster, yet discover spaces sprawling out before me, still and waiting to be explored. Within us, below the complicated surface and delving into the unseen, there is an expanse of open land calling out in quiet mystery. And this ground does not fade with time nor lay endlessly frozen, but holds within its enriching soil a taste of many springs to come.

The Powerful Light of Hope

At the end of the hall of darkness there is a light of hope that waits. For anyone who knows the internal pain of despair's bleak and isolating shadow, the ray from this glorious light is often seen as a faint glimmer, yet remarkably enduring. There is no fanfare, no grand announcement upon its arrival, for it seems it always was and tirelessly has always been, its origin as ancient as the stars shining with an ever-present glow within a vast and moving galaxy. It has held up and lasted throughout time despite the torments of life and amid our suffering it will continue to prevail, its resiliency tested and passed down as humanity's birthright. It is kept alive within us, and through our giving—however seen as large, however perceived as small—the power of hope offers its infinite light to all.

The truth is, your truth is what
your soul is ready to embrace.

SILENT CRIES TO BE KNOWN

Confined within a cycle of patterns are our silent cries to be known. Each time we become habitually upset over a recurring trigger. Each time we acquire another useless form of clutter to occupy the space which never seems to feel satisfied. Each time we become baffled and frustrated by our suffering and circumstance. What is the ultimate purpose if not to examine each emotional reactivity up close? What true longings are being held captive inside our incessant cravings…within our insatiable grasps for more? In this life, within us, is a song calling out to be released of its enclosure. When we begin digging with the deep-truth questions and listen to the honest answers we uncover, we gain a new freedom. Every discovery becomes an essential note extolling the beauty of our awakening song. And we can rejoice, at last, ungirded by old strife and think clearly. We needn't ever fear to delve further into self-knowing, where past the stratum of complexities awaits our soul's calming wisdom.

The late moon rises into a misty sky tonight,
and the entire world below in darkened slumber
within my view. Even when the nightfall grows
silently uncertain between the hours,
I will feel the gentle hope inside,
lifting me up and through the shadows—
forever, in its strong wings.

In the Truest of Places

I walk a new path on this late part of day, feeling at peace with the scenic trail and sharing the pulse of nature all around me. My thoughts are light enough to be carried along with the dove's airy call. I'm not feeling overwhelmed with finding the many penetrating answers to life's biggest questions. I don't feel any urgency to attend the latest seminar that will expose what is holding me back from discovering my personal truth. And I do not sense any need to seek and uncover the deepest of spiritual reason. Instead, I simply yield to settling into the heart of where I am, *right now*. Like a heron landing effortlessly to stand stoically in a pond. You learn in this life, there are times to go forth and search for meaning, just as there are times to be still and let meaning find you, exactly where you are, in the truest of places.

You are older now and say it is the winter of your life and impossible to ever find love. But the feeling you are capable of loving, that there is love in you and that love wants to move through you, that is what is most important. Inside you feel vibrant and alive and not past the peak moments of love. No, it is never too late to give love. And there is a time inside of each season for everything to find its true place.

Suddenly there was an opening, not conjured up or planned, where no longer did our defenses stand in strict command. With all guards now stripped away, resistance cannot withstand. We gave our vulnerable voice a chance to let our hearts speak out again.

LET THEM GO

Let them go,
all the leaves
once green regrets,
now sweet and rusted
wings of wisdom
floating on the
winds of reason.
Sweep them up
and craft a pile
shining with
imagination—
toss the sparks
into the air and
watch them
glow...

He won't define you,
complete you,
fix or redeem you.
He will be the one you'll want
to be real with in life
as he becomes all that he truly is.

You are the Greatest Guru

You are the greatest guru, the guiding light of each blessed day. You wash the dirty dishes, take out the trash and work the late shift. Yet within all the long hours, you see the glory in sharing and caring.

A spiritual life is not on the top of a distant mountain, nor is it inscribed in a prayer book of long ago. It is where you are inside your everyday when you've an open heart of love.

Sentient Scriptures of Truth

Spirituality doesn't arise from a ritual of reading from sacred text, but from simply partaking in the earthly connection we create with one another, while taking heartfelt steps towards sustaining the complexities within this living, breathing interconnectedness that is our beautiful planet home. It is not based on a cultural set of practices or rules of traditional belief placed before us, but about becoming well within ourselves, then reaching out to aid and assist others. And in doing so, we become sentient scriptures of truth at the close of each passing day.

LOVE IS ALWAYS

Its impact is not to be regarded any less than its mystery. We think about it. We chase after it. We search for it in the obscure places. We evade it sometimes, and at the same time we fear losing it when it finds us. No matter how often we meet it, it comes as a sudden surprise— its arrival unpredictable. As indefinable, we attempt to solidify it by reason and intention. We try to measure it, crack its code, then map out its perimeters. We lie awake at night because of it, giving it all our careful thought and restless attention. We are discovered by it, strengthened in it, drawn to the cadence of its beat, disheartened by its ebbing tide. Still, it is as constant as the entire sea, going nowhere and being everywhere at once, existing long before and surely ever after. We are broken open from it and mended carefully in it. Unveiled and revealed in it, tenderly healed by it. And just when we think that our growth has brought us to the place in which all is fully known, life will have taught us one more time: We can run from silenced pain and hide deeply in its shadow, but love is in there, too, with waiting arms wide open, standing patiently in line. *For love is always near, and far from being done with us yet.*

Go ahead soul, celebrate yourself. In this vast and moving world where you can easily feel small and inconsequential, understand and accept your great and undeniable importance. And though everyone and everything is surely headed for the void, one thing is certain: That you exist. Your memories, your experiences, and your essence will not ever be repeated.

Love does not break off pieces of a person
to fit another's empty spaces.

Those are for you to fill
as your love grows and entwines.

The Biggest Lie Your Ever Told

The biggest lie you ever told yourself
was that it was no big deal.

The tremendous cover up was when you
acted as if nothing ever happened.

The greatest survival tactic was to create a
convincing camouflage and hold it deep inside.

The ultimate decoy was to position yourself
as though you dealt with it once and for all.

Now the most compassionate thing you
can do for yourself is to come clean.

Expose the absolute truth and begin to mend
all the parts of you that were in on it.

Your heart. Your mind.
Your body and soul.

Integrity often takes the long way and has no interest in saving time. Her convictions are based on truth and having the courage to go the distance with the strong belief that she will reach her desired destination. So, if you're walking with integrity, you share a righteous, noble path. You may not get there first, but you will arrive honorably.

When at the end of this day,
if all you feel you can offer the world
is a handful of brokenness, give it.
Then in return, let the world hold you
in its grace as you sleep tonight.

For some, it takes time to fit comfortably into their own being and have a healthy regard for personal happiness and wellness. It takes a process to come to know self-worth, to feel individual power and potential and to grant the space to make changes for it to fully happen. Once there, self-love becomes a celebration of freedom to exist truthfully. Where there were once the dismal feelings of negativity and defeat, now shines a sterling shield reflecting unique beauty, passionate interests, and empowerment. Each spark inside joyfully ignites as the day's form of worship. And for you who profess you are not entirely feeling the drumfire of self-love, may you find your way into the sunlight where you can see you are loved, unabashedly and powerfully.

Everyone comes from somewhere. Everyone has a starting place and will eventually arrive at an end place. Though the path is not always linear or the way not entirely clear to see, we can be assured that each experience, each distraction, each event and everything in between is the content that makes life entirely worth living. What matters is what we pause to see, learn and discover along the way, and how we allow these marvelous interruptions to become our treasured memories. Life gives us the place, we are meant to dance in its space. Not expecting too much but appreciating the wonder when it comes into view, embracing different cultures, while continually learning about ourselves—eventually we come to understand the point of it all. To live. To sing. To feel the music being played. It won't always be easy, but it will be memorable and enriching. May you be blessed with all these things, be filled with this simple, glorious wonder and let your song play loud and true.

The logic of my mind will never fully understand
the reasoning of my heart.

There came a time in my life when fatigue arrived as a chronic messenger to my body and soul, tugging on my busy sleeve each day, nearly every waking hour, imploring me to become inactive, urging me to seek repose. Anyone who knows the seriousness of exhaustion understands the debilitation it can lead to, often to the point of becoming physically ill or in pain for days at a time. It was difficult to admit because I equated busyness with accomplishment. But as I listened to my body, I learned that rest is as vital as activity and I could not develop healthily while depleting myself entirely. Eventually I accepted resting as part of the growth experience. I can appreciate how it allows me to recover, revitalize and rekindle—and when I take time to rest, I will not become irrelevant, I will not fall behind in my journey. Now I welcome the ease of space and am grateful to my persistent messenger.

LOVE RELEASED IN A NEW WAY

Let the love that dwells inside
be released in a new way.
Let it out and let it flow in each
direction of your innermost terrain.
Let it sweep and fill old pains
and empty cases,
let it spill into the storage pile
of agonizing places.
Like the moment when you should
have left, but stayed.
Or that time you felt like forfeiting, yet remained.
Let it run through the corridors of your life story,
then up its stairs in search for wistful memories.
Let it expose where all your precious grace
and healing treasures lay.
Let the love you keep inside
come out to be with you, today.

I believe in angels and I can see them all around. Benevolent beings, ministering spirits and inspirers of goodness. They always hold the door for those who carry heavy loads. They help friends in sudden need and read to young children. They rescue unwanted animals, deliver food to the shut-in, bring warm blankets to the shelters, and volunteer their smile to a passing lonely soul. They're an encouragement to the disheartened, reassurance to the timid, and a comfort to the sick. I believe in angels and I see them every day, doing selfless acts from a caring heart that makes the world a better place.

The evening feels into a steady calm. The black veiled sky relies on its amber moon. I sit and think openly tonight, while the moon is present and forgiving. It's been two weeks since my father passed away from this world and now both of my parents are gone. I feel breakable in the sweet frailty of being an old child. To anyone who is grieving, allow yourself to feel whatever comes through your soul. Grant yourself time to experience whatever it is you need to undergo this delicate, vital transition. If you find you are becoming acutely aware of the quality and quantity of your life, then be graceful with yourself. Be sympathetic and soft towards your spirit as you would be to a tender child. And be as present and forgiving as the moon in amber glow.

A New Approach

Take a moment to be real then settle into the absence of any existing restraints. No commitment to meet anyone, no urgency to be somewhere. The arrival of a fresh year is gracefully nearing and it is not asking for any resolution, nor begging for you to do better. It simply wants to invite you into its presence and make of it what you will. No need to worry, no cause to fret. No requirements to fill or conditions to be met. No more strict promises or guilt. No needless pressure, no sweat. Try a new approach to a different year: Let time be an encouraging mother and her daughters a blessing of honest days.

Three Dancers

It's not that we must continually insist on moving, looking, and thinking in strictly forward motions, but to also recognize that the great basis for life is its repeating notes. The rise and fall. The patterned flow. The recurring beats. And that we go on to observe how out of devastation comes new birth and maintenance. The soul who knows this is like the ecstatic artist, capable of foreseeing a time when beauty will arise from the ruins. They are the one whose inspirited hands pluck the remnants of grace from out of the wreckage. They are forever enheartened knowing joy and sorrow step hand in hand, while they anticipate the perfections and imperfections of existence within this consonance song. And because somewhere inside the intervals of time, in between hardship and amid celebration, they learned how the forces of destruction, creation, and preservation weave in and out of one another as intimate dance partners in the rhythm of life.

What are you carrying that you need not? Are you holding onto something that makes you not want to take risks, open yourself to create, but in their place bear the intense pain of regret? Shame is such a harsh taskmaster, and guilt its evil twin. Letting go is not always as easy as it sounds, but you can do it just the same. Allow the tender hearts of those who love you become the light that guides you towards self-forgiveness. You honor yourself when you give your hands of creation back to love.

Recovery is a long and challenging road paved with hope and second chances. You are going to make it up the hills and through each valley because you are working on your stuff this time, taking it one day, one choice, one triumph, and one courageous step at a time.

A Vital Spark in Nature

I often contemplate the ritual coding in nature with its hidden systems of communication and its spiritual significance that allows us to reconnect with our truest self. Let the wilderness both teach and bear witness that the life force within knows instinctively just who you are, is aware of your place in the glory of Earth, and perceives the natural gifts held inside. Let the wilderness guide you to understanding your interconnectedness. For when you come to learn the unity of all things, you no longer feel compelled to change your shape or take on new forms to fit the expectations of what you think others might envision you to be. You will recognize yourself. You will know who you are and trust you're akin to the Great Circle and will embrace your role in its preservation and the offering of your innate gifts. And if you ever need reminding, *go back.* Go back to the mountains and the trees, the dirt and the moss, the sands and the wind, the mist and the deer, who call forth your deep connection and inborn intuition. You are undeniably a vital spark within all of nature, here to be alive more fully and wholly, with creation's wisdom dwelling also in you. Let this be among your greatest of enlightenments.

What if one day you come to the realization that you never again have to explain yourself away to anyone anymore, or that you no longer must carry the burden of another's false perception of you or your own perceived inadequacies and you could relax, finally, in knowing you're incredible in the light you are standing in at this moment. And what if you go on to not care about the judgments someone else might have—that your life is not full or amazing enough—or that you no longer feel the need to endlessly apologize for being human?

That day has been graciously waiting for you to begin swimming in its warm waters of love and acceptance.

Let's walk in this world, you and I, together. Let's be explorers of the sacred every day. We will voyage into the heart matters to compare what we learn and have yet to figure out, then gently collapse inside the mystery of what we may never understand. Let's be pilgrims in a land of prismatic doors to be opened, and we'll savor each realization that steps through. We'll be life's devoted pupils, asking questions religiously, discerning glimpses of truth in one another's eyes. And you won't insist you own every answer, and I won't pretend to be holding all the keys. For you are ever the enlightened one in the acceptance of not infinitely knowing...and I will always be the seeker, not the one who claims the way.

Your Words are Keys

Write them out.
Your words are keys
to free what is even now within you—
sheer doubts and shy whispers
waft above a deeper knowing.
Sweep out the waiting corners,
dust off the forgotten shelves
to find the clues,
and write them down.
Your hopes, your fears.
Your eyes will clear.
The cage will open
in recognition of your truth.

I think the most beautiful thing about a lasting love is how two people learned to believe in one another. They know it's never about trying to make the other person happy. They understand it's not about needing to be attractive by cultural standards. And they recognize it's not ever at all about being seduced by enticements that will inevitably fade away. It's in the way they coalesce, sharing gentle discoveries of the other one's honesty as they uncover each truth of their own. It's how they burned the midnight oil over time to get to a place of such luminous faith and trust. As if long ago both souls clasped hands in dedication to live in authenticity and love, and became devoted to relishing the sweetness of their truth. They're solid now. There will still be storms in the night, but they can ride them out until the dawn breaks light—because they really learned to believe in one another. *They believe.*

The Secret Godsend

See and recognize the secret godsend that is in every second, the perfect shining moment realized, because the most favorable of all blessings are contained within you and within me being here. Whether doing our personal best or exceeding our foremost efforts, we all share the same valuable time, space and worth. We are in this, right here and now, together. And who we are, what we do and will become, will glow radiantly through each one of our remarkable steps on this earth.

THE GREATEST WORK IN PROGRESS

The greatest thing you can do
is to become who you are
and not allow the parts
of what make you
a complete individual—
your creative energies,
your valued interests, and
your unique strengths and passions—
to wither away from neglect
or be repressed by whoever
or whatever surrounds you.

You are a masterpiece
and a great work in progress.

You carry within you an ocean called love, its depth I cannot fathom. Understanding how grief is a part of love's profundity does not make the pain of loss any less excruciating, but you will have walked through a new point of entry. You will remember its connection to love, with each step, and go on.

KISS THE INEFFABLE BLISS

At some point in life you will look back on your journey and may ask yourself the question, *which part mattered to me the most?* Yes, life gave way to some unexpected pain at times when there was just no stomach for it. The heartache of grief felt like a concrete cross you had to carry over mountains. Then there were days you learned about things the hard way, feeling the sting of regret a time or two, although you may not care to admit it. Even so, you're likely to treasure each triumphant victory and playfully recall the twinkling markers of time. Because you were blessed to be uplifted and became familiar with being let down. You walked through fire and danced with elation. And though you may have stumbled more times than you can count, you held the space and kept the faith. All the while, with a fearless and tenacious heart, you forged ahead, holding everything and everyone you ever loved inside a precious world where gratitude spread like blooming wildflowers alongside gushing streams of joy. Even when it hurt you persevered, as your light burned fiercely and bright. It wasn't all for naught, and in the end, you'll embrace the entire panorama and kiss the ineffable bliss as you declare the final answer: *I lived. And it ALL mattered. Every. Single. Moment.*

Sensitive soul, what are you holding in that detains you from moving on, or keeps you from trying again? Are you carrying the weight of his words on your back? Are her curses still echoing the halls of your heart? Here's the key point, although at one time those heartless put downs and insensitive remarks broke in and crushed your spirit, their words have no authority to remain. Don't let them reside in your temple nor allow them freedom to paralyze your mind. Instead, when someone's unkind criticism attempts to claim you, let this become a pivotal moment by denying those words air or space. Perhaps they will perish, or maybe even go back to the mouth that spilled them. It really doesn't matter, because from now on you will nourish your spirit with empowering words that will take you higher in your life's callings.

I used to view faith from afar, as if it were an invisible element I must reach for, and which could make the impossible feel conceivable. I once held the notion faith was reserved for those who appealed to an unseen power for a miraculous outcome. I have since learned faith was in me all along and could easily be scattered outward like small seedlings each day, and would grow over time into monumental things. I learned the real marvel of faith is ensconced within our trust and belief that goodness holds the power to prevail as we live in the day-after-day with one another, and when we manage to overcome the obstacles set before us to gain an understanding. When we decide to help someone without expecting anything in return. When we speak out against injustice. When we offer no unfair judgments. And when the shadows emerge, we learn from them as we lean in towards the light of love. That itself is a miracle of faith like no other.

You've been shattered. Yet, the amazing thing isn't that heartbreak may have made you stronger or that it was better for you to have had the chance to love than not at all. It's despite all that happened, despite all your wounds, your gentle heart is still alive inside and continues to beat among the shards—and how you miraculously trust in its rhythm to guide your steps back over to love.

Welcome anything new arising from within you, that which was always there but had not been expressed. Welcome all the parts of you that have waited and longed to begin forming and grow joyously into view.

You are not a coward. You have walked into the countless firestorms of life that would make the knees of a champion shudder at the very sight. You raised a child and held the hand of a dying loved one. You pulled from every inner resource to keep an entire family functioning and fed. *You are not a coward.* You once hit the bottom of a dark pit only to climb out to greet the light of the next transition. You didn't need nerves of steel or pray for superhuman strength, but relied on a determined heart of love to live your life for something big.

There are times when the exact words we want to say to express our deeper meaning are suddenly unavailable, or all at once become non-existent. At best, they may falter on their way out, stammering only half of what we truly feel or may fall away to be lost in translation. But when we finally connect with the rare ones who we are blessed to call kindred spirits, it will be our hearts that end up doing most of the talking. And it will be within our silences that we can hear what is hidden inside our souls.

The wind also carries in its gust a seed of hope, both powerful and gentle, reminding that new things can begin, take root and grow after the cyclone of events or sudden gale of destruction set you back. And with renewed dedication, this tendril will continually thrive in the warm light of life, its leaves flourishing inside each fresh, invigorating morning.

Our soul will speak our deepest yearnings that we long to convey to another. We search for steady hands where we can delicately place our innermost desires to be held in protected trust, then form an unfaltering cup with our own to offer the very same. The mere thought of this intimate exchange can unearth our most subterranean fears. But when we become consciously caring and yield to the nature of love, we create a perfect sanctuary of tenderness and safety where we can express the wants and the needs kept within.

TIMELESS BEING

Sometimes you're not entirely sure where to fit in, just how to be, or exactly where you belong. It's so hard to squeeze inside all their tight spaces at just the right interval. You're ahead of your time and too pure for the future, yet in this moment unrestricted you find the innermost place that is true to your very being and where you shine unforgettably. So… keep becoming who you are, timeless being, for this momentary world needs such endless beauty that is *you*.

Bless you for being noble, for being tolerant and kind. For turning the other cheek while waiting patiently void of conditions in a never-ending line. Know this, you too are worthy of not being put off until tomorrow in love's eyes. You don't need to do better to be held in love's unquestionable embrace. And you don't ever have to stand by or be detained from entering love's room, but can walk in and be seen anytime, night or day.

I Threw Off My Prayer Beads

I threw off my prayer beads
to become an answer to prayer.
I stopped confessing my sins
to banish guilt and despair.
I found a compassionate heart
refusing rituals that were vain.
I ceased chanting into emptiness
to hear the ones who cry in pain.
And now love is my ceremony,
nature, my guide—
and my mantra is to embrace
my ever-abundant life.

One-of-a-Kind Spirit

Sometimes the one with the most astonishing and gentle power, the most breath-taking beauty, and the most resolute heart is passed by and may never appear as obvious to the onlooker because they don't need or call out for trivial attention. Yet to the observant and the keen, this one-of-a-kind spirit is a great blessing. And right before their eyes emerges a work of genius and pure magic like no other.

It was often during your weakest moments that grace appeared to benevolently bestow the profound strength to keep your heart open. You know what it's like to feel torn inside, and through tending to your own wounds you learned to have self-compassion then continued with a genuine and caring sensitivity for others. There are none who pass through this life unscathed. No, not even one. And without being wounded, how would we ever be able to care and empathize without reservation? How else would we otherwise learn?

The heart's cry to be seen is perhaps even greater than the fundamental need for acceptance. Taking time to acknowledge another by simply looking at them with warmth, or even an act of kindness is so much better than looking past them. Your littlest smile can lift a heavy heart. For when you truly see and affirm another, you are magnifying a soul's worthy presence.

THE CURRENT OF MYTH

What are the stories that are holding you up, locking you in, and leaving you to feel left behind? What are the epic lies that have kept you bound? Although you may feel surrounded by tales of distortion, your confidence is well within you, residing in your soul, preserved by love and patience. The more you resist and reject the rapids of self-deceit and step up to the truth of your birth—that you are here and you belong—the easier it becomes for all the untruths and all the false stories to fall into the current of myth and be washed away as forgotten. And as the shadows of fiction are being replaced with honesty and compassion, the glorious light of confidence within your spirit will emerge in full swing as you move freely.

Let heartbreak be the initiation into
the divine halls within you.

We are lights rightly placed and created to shine with pride. I do not say this in a way that diminishes humility, but in a spirit that uplifts humanity. This light is not meant to be judged as an imposing beam of brash and arrogance. Rather, it is a remarkable presence that is the essence of human dignity possessing the true power of humility—not held higher or lower but placed among to understand the presence of another. It is each one's divinity to belong.

O glorious life!
Each moment holds

radiant meaning,
as if an entire sea of stars,

and is just as divine
as it is humbling.

Go Where the Heartpain Leads

If you go where the heart-pain leads, you may risk entering the deep caverns of a secret world where meandering shadows converge with pure light, among layers of metamorphous, yet unfolding. And if you follow the heart's wanting cry, you might find fossils formed long ago near grottos of crystal clear streams. You'll see gypsum glowing white near colossal stalagmites, rising from the depths of your emotional holdings. Fiery crimson stone hues swirl with vibrational blues inside scar tissue and tear-soaked ravines. If you go where the pangs want to lead, you may chance finding a profound heart restoration when you emerge.

It seems contrary to what one would intuitively expect to imagine kindness and power as strong and able companions. Understanding your ability to maintain kindness for yourself and others is what is cultivating your emotional strength and allowing more positive feelings to take root, thus building inner resiliency over time. Step by step, day by day it becomes easier to overcome many of life's obstacles as the miraculous makes its appearance through kindness every day. One gesture at a time, one caring heart at a time, we become builders of kindness, laying the foundation for a better world. Compassionate people are incredibly powerful people.

The best part of the worst times in my life was the concomitant storm that would gather within. Thunder waving through the dark clouds and lightening breaking the limits of my horizon—and everything got soaked inside. Ultimately, I'd crash into an outcropping of a new conviction that would be my solid rock, and when it's all over I remember how each trial and struggle can be the spark of all my awakenings, and how I'm never really the same after the rains.

I'm reborn after each storm.

The Stuff of Heroes

Don't ever tell her she's not the stuff of heroes and warriors simply because she's a girl. Don't ever imply she's weak or too delicate to overcome. She is a resilient being of flesh and light, the epitome of beauty—made up of thoughts and intellect, endurance and courage, her essence as unique as her dreams. She'll tear away thorny vines and scale walls to climb her way through adversity. She'll arise to challenge and will eat all the *what ifs* before they ever have a chance to consume her. She will go places. And everywhere she goes, the stars will be suffused by her shine.

Paradox

It's not that you must strive to always feel certain, but instead to become open. Open with a mind led by curiosity and receptiveness to welcome that which appears illogical or self-contradictory. You may very well feel vulnerable walking through such incongruent terrain, but it can be an unexpected positional point for growth and learning. Accepting yourself in this place and developing from here is part of the adventure.

Society demands we immediately conform, perhaps, and conformity doesn't quite allow ample space for trying new things and self-development. At times, we need to stir the waters and make mistakes as we experiment our way towards what feels personally comfortable. Society is filled with the artificial among pretense and hypocrisy. Fitting in is not important, but finding yourself—truly settling into your being-ness—is paramount.

Like a sweet morning mist rising from the churning lake, our truth finds its way up out from our uncertainty. I think the phases when we feel most uncomfortable, absolutely awkward, clumsy and graceless and not quite our real selves are the times when the most authentic and best parts within can emerge as a wonderfully revealing surprise.

The Liminal Phase

You must not retreat on your journey just because it ceases to make any sense feeling lodged in the in-between. Yes, there may come a time when a liminal phase is unappealing or even discouraging, your identity suddenly a puzzle, and clinging to a former phase seems to be the only familiar thing to grasp hold of. Yes, it might even feel bewildering and ambiguous walking in the middle of two of life's chapters—not really old, not very young. Neither high nor low, rather, fixed upon a lengthy threshold before a noble rite of passage. The impulse to defy your present category, or resume a past persona, or take up completely new traits to clarify your whereabouts will rush in to assist you, and that can be all right. Be reassured, it is all part of the human experience, even this place called the In-Between. And you can take your time within this space. You can contemplate the deeper meanings you missed as an adolescent. You can try new things and gain broader emotional range. You can dive into the mosaic seas of your innerscapes and surface with sparkling treasure. You can be playful inside your second youth and wise within your years. Most importantly, you can keep living your bold and valiant life... even while you're feeling confused.

Fall in love with yourself. Settle down into the truth of your existence—that you matter. Make a commitment to self-empowerment. Be in a relationship with self-worth. Don't make bids for love and attention in places where there is no genuine interest. Rather, go where you're joyfully acknowledged as you make a vow to cherish your deserving and precious life.

The world is full of troublemakers that make our planet a safer place. Some got arrested for protesting threats facing the precious environment. Others were cited for marching against the menace of war. And many served time for objecting to inequality. For every person throughout the ages who stepped forth to denounce corruption, violence and injustice, we salute you with our hearts, for we know the real and great offender is that which tries to rob us of our peace while here on earth.

Glory to the small steppers, slow-and-steady growers, shy believers and the quietly determined dreamers who attend to others along their way. They are not found on a quest towards the limelight, caught usurping all the credit, or ever exposed as needing to run the entire show. They don't own the obstinate final say, shout blaring opinions or slam down needless ultimatums. In fact, you may barely notice them, for they already possess a sweet inner confidence to move in the direction of their aspirations while silently helping those all around. They are patient within themselves and never make waves to get attention and praise. If ever you are blessed to know one like this, stop to give them the honor their altruistic soul deserves. Applaud their wisdom to move with careful assurance, bow to their humbleness to be a leader who'll serve.

I don't believe in magic, but I do believe in super powers. I think it is possible to transmute the primary fears that block us, along with any residual pain that's collected from our life experiences, into actively positive energy if we are willing to take an honest look and do the work required for transforming ourselves into liberated and empowered beings. We become alchemic heroes. Heroes save their self, discover their purpose, achieve balance and ultimately increase their happiness. We can all become heroes. And of all our marvelous achievements, allowing ourselves to live in the sacredness of our personal, sweet truth is our most meritorious.

Hate is the abomination, not sexual orientation.

In-Bodying Spirituality

Maybe we stood and gazed at a colorful picture of spirituality as something outside of the body. Maybe we embraced a concept told by perfect masters of enlightened thought, who talk at times to the point of complete separation from the body and exclusively achievable by some, but not inclusive to everyone. The truth is we all possess the capacity to be aware of our connections to one another in this life. We can all interface with what we sense and recognize as God-energy. We all hold the choice to reach out and be present with any living being in any way we can at any moment, by any means. It is within you and it's within me. We are the perfect threads of relational time— woven in close, side-by-side. And the extent, the amount, or the level of our ability to be present cannot be calculated or measured. We *are* perfect. None are too frail or too far, viewed as insufficient or perceived as incidental, discounted as remote or too inconsequential to become an essential and binding thread in the weave of this majestic cloth covering all.

Heal at your own gentle pace. Be caring and patient. Little by little, the hurt becomes less enduring. You'll always remember, and maybe wince from time to time, but I can tell you it gets better when applying care to your tender emotional cuts and scrapes.

THE BALM OF HEALING

The Balm of Healing
Contains: compassion,
honesty, and awareness.

When using: Remove all denial
from source of wound and cleanse affected
area with awareness to induce recognition
and insight. Apply compassion generously
and wherever there is any sign of pain.
Distribute honesty liberally throughout
entire process, being sure to absorb
all unnecessary stories and false beliefs.

Reapply compassion as often as needed.

Marriage is not restrictive to being between a man and a woman; rather, marriage is hands aligned, safely holding two hearts in truth and love.

Hallucinations of the Soul

The longing for things that you could not have, the yearning for places you were not destined to arrive. Wistful memories of what was not ever meant to be. Regret for not being who you thought you would become. These hallucinations of the soul are agonizing prisoners that must be pardoned and released. Clear the room. Open the door and let them leave.

And in this space, you'll paint a glorious existence of being here with presence and contentment for what truly is a relevant and meaningful life.

My Bare-Skinned Soul

Who am I under the skin? Each person has so many protective coverings. Layers and layers wrapped around the core. Penetrating layers of what has happened, what is happening, what we perceive and who it is we believe ourselves to be. Then there is the superficial veneer decoratively sealing everything underneath. Maybe we know so much when it comes to the topical aspects around us that we can gradually become unfamiliar with our bona fide self among it all. To deeply know myself, to distinguish my pure and concentrated essence, I understood what had to be done. I had to go under. And by lifting each veil that had been withstanding then working through the assortment of coatings, one at a time, I could expose the original portal. The gateway that would take me directly into my own earth. And each time I get closer to the internal network of roots, I get to know my bare skinned soul.

It takes a certain strength to hold it all in.
It takes even more strength to speak out.
And the voice that speaks from a wounded heart
is not ineffectual or cowardly, however faint the cry.

While our spiritual necessities are essential, we must also strive to become dedicated and attuned to the must-haves outside the soul. The physical house, the body, requires attention and upkeep, just as we do for the spiritual temple. We must endeavor to prioritize our offering for those lacking food, shelter, clothing, and education. In the spiritual world, the least are recognized as the greatest. Devotion is only significant when concomitant with love for all sacred life, compassionately engaged and in harmony with both the spiritual and material needs alike.

Don't linger in the need to impress anyone while there's an entire world of impressions all around you waiting and in need of your delight. In the very details of nature—in the rain puddles soaking into the ground, the soft forming clouds, the baby grasshopper clinging to its sweet blade. The dandelion that creates its own seed as a means of recreating itself.

Each and every sunrise holds the richness of life, and whatever was before becomes a part of the ongoing impact and beauty of the natural world... *reminding you of being alive.*

Knowing when to make fair concessions and being agreeable to compromise becomes a practice to be perfected, balancing your giving side without sacrificing or overlooking the vital personal obligations to self. The gentle-hearted by nature, the easygoing dispositions, and the mild-mannered sensitive ones have endured the tantrums of playmates demanding they bring out all their special toys only to be left alone to pick up after playtime. To feel abandoned after giving all you have within can leave you gasping with emptiness. Keep yourself in the picture, you matter. Never concede yourself away in any situation. You must cherish your song so everyone else can hear it and join in sweet harmony.

The Affirming Language of Poetry

Poetry is ever beautifully defined by a myriad of vital souls. Communication, either spoken or written, attempts to seize reality and connect. Thoughts encoded are relayed to be decoded. Feelings, concepts, ideas. The images swirling within the depths of our being, forming lines, shaping into words, everything held so embryonically tight unfolds its limbs as a new language is birthed that we knew not before. A poem must be conceived within each soul before it is born into the world. And it is Poetry that invites anyone and everyone to come out with personal expression using words forming lines, patterned schemes set to feeling, meters and beats, freestyle or rhyme...all validating the human existence.

To realize your essential self—the core of your magnificent essence—all the favored illusions collected and held securely in place must come undone. To become fully aware requires a stripping down of every layered misconception seeded around the soul. To know *the you right now* is to make the clear distinction separate from another, silence the mind prattle and comprehend the moment. To realize yourself, *uncover all your darling misconceptions and bring your authentic light on through…*

FIRE INSIDE YOUR SOUL

You polished the crown of your essence during one of the most intense trials of your life. When all the seams came undone and you stood alone in the fray, with no one in sight or any relief to be found, you awoke to lift yourself out of bed to take on the next day. The lesson wasn't the trial itself; it wasn't the disaster or the storm. It wasn't being knocked down, pressed in, shaken up or overwhelmed. It was how you reached into the bowels of your being and fastened to the ground. You walked between not wanting to believe in God and not wanting to give up believing, so you could have someone to blame or someone to cry out to. You just didn't want to feel alone. Even so, you latched on tighter to the cause as you firmly held your own. Taking no shortcuts, you went the entire way and refused to quit, while this thing inside kept forming—call it resilience, *call it grit*. You went from the surface into the depths with it, from the struggle into the sublime. And you didn't have to search in the dark because it was within you all that time. Now the very thing you need to understand about this fire inside your soul: No one can take away what turns the lead to solid gold.

Some people intentionally live an existence of unending disproportion with a lack of harmony and may not even recognize a healthier balanced lifestyle if it landed square on the head and centered them. Meanwhile, you mustn't live within another person's extremes. Recognize that balance is an art to be individually mastered over time. Come to appreciate your own personal challenges to achieve a sense of secure and even footing in the pace of all things.

So even after the embarrassing mishap, the sloppy communication, the fuzzy boundary, and the sore misunderstanding, love yourself with extra tenderness and care. And love yourself in the dark and uncertain spaces. Within these places, too, are the steps that lead you towards wholeness.

LASTING IMPRESSION

You leave the sheerest grains of yourself in scattered locations and zones. Droplets fall from your essence—only to land in hidden spaces, unknown. You held objects and things, all soon forgotten, while I held you secure in the most thoughtful places. Because what proved to endure, prolific and pure, is when you pressed your heart quietly into mine, and to this day its sweet imprint remains. And I will carry you there, your thin, sweet lasting impression.

DOUBLE STARS

There are two types of double stars.
The pair that appear close,
but are in fact at different distances
and are an optical double.

And there is the binary.
The pair that are mutually attracted
and bound to one another
by the forces of gravity and motion.

You must find your counterpoint in the heavens.

When I become heartbroken from a loved one's demise, I try to remember that life is fleeting for all and to love in the time allotted. This, too, is a small comfort but one nevertheless. Because I know stars die all the time, and for each one that dies one is born. Life continues so love may endure.

When you listen to people tell their story, they will invariably recount what they have gained in life and what it is they lost. Maybe there will be some who'll boast about how they worked diligently for years without much extravagance to attain such a beautiful home. Perhaps there'll be those who'll confess how they once sold their prized possessions to get through a hard time. Some will speak openly about leaving everything behind to seize a life of opportunities and taste the sweetness of freedom in a different land. And some may whisper sorrowfully how they lost a precious child. It's been said for everything we gain, we lose something else. I don't know if that's accurately true, but I know for certain that we will never get back everything. And so, the most stirring part of our story is how we willingly take that risk when we decide to live and we choose to love.

The Giving Loom

As a child, I always felt it a strange remedy being told to give as a way to uplift my spirits. In my child's mind, hearing people remark on how good it personally feels to give sounded like selfishness, as if it were all about the giver's need to feel a sense of validation. As I matured, I came to understand that what they were expressing carries a much deeper meaning and value than what it presented to me on the surface. *To give is to contribute to life*. To give affirms our existence. When we spare the time to listen to and talk with someone, we are engaging our hearts and are giving. Giving takes on a multitude of forms outside the obvious. Playing musical instruments, creating art, making meals, tending the garden. Teaching. Smiling at someone. Praying for another's well-being. In such we mingle within a cycle inside a universal loom, our essence blends and unites with others as interwoven threads of generosity creating a network that has a respiration all its own. To give creates a perpetual circle that comes back around to present itself for us to joyfully inhale with sweet reception. Giving also serves to remind the giver of the importance of their gift. Around it goes, and on it goes. To live is to give. To give is to live. And living and giving feels profoundly good inside.

GATHER ALL THE FOND MEMORIES

Gather all the fond memories
that settled deep inside you—
sweep them up with the fallen leaves,
the *if only's* and dry branches.
Visions you had when you were younger,
the *what might have beens* and lost chances.

Place them in your heart once more
and let them burn with sweet new smoldering.
Rekindling hope of autumn's spice mingling
with the playful wind
will tickle old wishful dreams
and breathe them back
to life again.

From our very first stages of development we began to form, grow and evolve. And throughout the many phases were moments in which we felt we've fallen short because what we chose to do or what we could only find in ourselves to do at any given time may not have measured up to someone's expectation. We must not see one another as insufficient or think of ourselves as being defeated in this magnificent process of change called *life*. Each decision is a step in the journey, a part of our story in the pages of time. And within each one of these steps, we will continue to develop and unfold, finding a greater sense of who we are and discerning the limits of what we can endure.

You broke into pieces, were torn into untold fragments, only to learn that you had so much more to you than ever conceived of before. And each priceless part of your being is worth gathering up the scattered remnants, picking out the painful splinters to be held in loving eyes.

It can feel emotionally tempting to remain numb after the shock of violence and terror. It's understandable to fall into the shadows of despair. We must in times of onslaught and barbarity remember to hold fast to love. Together we have walked through the broken halls of this life and witnessed contempt's power to destroy. Yet we likewise know, and have experienced in our lives, how love has an invincible courage and determination of its own. And all the love we carry individually will join forces to have the final say. Love will make an outcast of hate. Love will be the vindicator of fear's death wish. So, when your heart is gripped by way of terror and fear, reach out to one another and remember to connect. Remember to share. Remember to hold one another up in support and to care. Hold on and fasten to each other with love.

Each of us possess a gripping life story. A continuance of vital passages. An entire account of our earthly evolution. Each story is a relevant thread in this infinite weave of multicolored hue. Not every story will be spoken aloud. But every story is sacred. Every story worth recounting. Every story true. We must recognize the short-lived and silent threads, for they are part of the magnificent cosmic shawl. We must pause to give them a voice, to allow their spirit to take space to confess their existence. We must give them the honor that is due.

The Holiness in *I Will*

The power to choose your own actions, your purpose strengthened by your determination; your will is just as important as your desire to please. Being overly amenable or dutifully nice to the point of burying your will serves none in the end and might only entomb your spirit.

Your kind heart is in just the right place when it remembers to include you as the leading light. And soon you'll believe and ultimately understand:

There is holiness when saying the words *I will*.

In the darkest hour of desperation, hope is alive and working the late shift. When the nights become a shroud of despair, hope is on the job, ready to pierce through the heaviest of gloom. And when there's nothing left to take hold of—when every other emotion has been exhausted and there's nothing left in sight...hope rises out of despondency as a white beacon in a lightless room.

Sacred Core

I've been told that deep within me is a
godly essence, under coverings galore.
And to reach this holy center I must
expose the veils and let them fall.
But I can't discount each layer
wrapped around this sacred core.
Or the layers within the layers,
where dwells divinity inside of all.

LOVE EVERY PART OF YOU

Love every part of you.
Yes, the spaces and gaps
where you're still
in-between.
Love your trying,
your challenges,
your successes, your wins.
Love the distance you go,
love the places you're seen.

When I look at faith, I don't view an idealistic or notional idea of how things will exist, like in a fantasy or a disproportionate and unbalanced attempt to seize truth. When I look at faith, I don't see an insistent denial of facts or an angel of contradiction. When I look at faith, what I see instead is what stands up when certainty and morale shrink back in disbelief, then confidently walks up to the situation to offer an entirely new and believable reality. Faith will give me something palpably true to hold on to when there isn't anything I can be sure of to grasp firmly within sight. When I look at faith, I see myself holding a very real and intuitive knowing kept alive in fresh belief.

I think in the end it could be said we wanted the same.

We all wanted to be lights.

We all just want to be seen.

No matter the length we're to shine,
in that time we all yearn to be known.

So I see you my star, just as you are.

Know you should be loved.
You should be held safe and warm
inside an invested and caring heart.
You should walk away from
destructive and depleting forces
and walk alongside calming streams.
Know your dignity is deserving
of the loving places you belong.

Know that you matter
and should be loved.

You waited for it. You waited for him and you waited for her to make up their minds to deliver. You waited for the moment to show up and relieve you from holding everything upon your shoulders. Now it is up to you, because waiting for someone else to make it happen for you is not likely. Sometimes when we no longer want to believe in something we can really have, we stop looking for it, and instead create a zone of comfort where we soothe the loss of what we were never given and never took the risk to find out for ourselves. To hinder your own what-could-be, or prevent your expansion and personal growth by remaining in a self-imposed hide-out of limitations and compression is like never planting beautiful flowers because you're uncertain about the possibility of seeing them flourish. You're worth taking the necessary risk of becoming actualized and blossoming. You're worth doing it for yourself.

Love Will Find its Way In

It takes courage for someone to confront their phobias and delve into the deep recesses of their darkest fears to gain an understanding. It's not always an apparent maneuver to select love over fear, as if to suggest it were that simple, or as if it is the only option to plainly weigh. For often it is not enough to simply say, *"Love will conquer all fear"*, until you know and have done the work around the personal irrationalities that have been hindering love's complete entrance. Your negative fear can instead be calmed by tenderness and patience, and to make a full recovery you must be willing to excavate your heart and mindset. You must be willing to dig with raw and penetrating questions, and be prepared for what honest truths are uncovered. By doing so, you are removing each stone stacked against you, preventing you from perfect love, breaking through the barriers that have been built over time by trauma or circumstance. All the while, as you are being self-compassionate in this endeavor, love is permeating the spaces fear formerly inhabited. And in time love will release the remaining hostages of hate, panic and anxiety and saturate them with grace and mercy as they transform into light and forgiveness. Damaging fear will dissipate as it is therapeutically acknowledged...*and love will find its way in.*

Bless Your Mistakes

The constant questioning of your intuition. Discrediting your life experience. It all happens inside the fear of making mistakes and being trapped in its confinements. The lingering unease before stepping out to make weighty decisions may always be present, but you were never meant to be motionless in life. You are not destined to become hindered from living, not attuned to your instincts, preserved in a frozen block of fear. Begin to bless your mistakes as noble attempts to explore and expand as a human being. Trust yourself once again. Soon you will no longer ignore your core, but begin seizing all the valuable insight and discovery birthed out of your very own wonderfully revealing mistakes.

Unlock all the windows
of your soul tonight—
push away your indecision,
then open wide.
Let the papers scatter,
let the curtains fly.
And the dreams
you tucked away,
wake them up
to play outside.

You are the Mystic

You are the mystic,
set among the unseeing,

whirling in passion first believed,
fused in patterns of deep meaning.

Breathe in and stretch out,
all your senses entranced.

Skirts swirling all about, as your
purpose becomes the dance.

An important part of stepping into your growth and actualization is identifying when you're obscuring the light of your purpose by habitually putting everyone else's needs or requests before your own. Your love for others is not ever in question, gentle heart. When you serve, let your decisions flow from an authentic and honorable well. Lift the veil of false offerings that lead to pleasing a vessel that only grows to hold resentment, depletion, guilt and exhaustion. And by doing so, you will have given yourself one of the greatest of things: The room to grow honestly.

NIGHT SKY

I'll never tire of the sky at night, or become disenchanted with how it perfects an entire evening in arrays of glowing white. Looking up, I see the stars ever in conflict, constantly pulling inward yet shining forth like lucent diamonds streaming down with sweetest light. And Orion stretches out its spiral arm across the vastness of our galaxy, holding all within its care. As silent embers watching over me, my guardians swim in heaven's seas. That I am part of this majesty, this awesome starlit wonder, fills my heart with sheer amazement where beams a smile of pure delight.

Music is the reflective language between the finite and infinity. Utterly sublime and divine, it miraculously sees into our very souls and lifts us higher. The sounds we can project are innumerable. Each note we release drifts through our heart's many heavens and finds its way back to God.

THREE THINGS

There are three things that
will come to you like
an unforeseen revelation
in the course of your journey:

The magnitude of the final straw,
the unexpected person who teaches
you the true meaning of compassion,
and your astonishing capacity to love
in this one and only life.

They call it *Firgun*. It's that feeling when something quite good happens to someone other than yourself, yet their blessing collides with your heart only to get tangled up in pure and honest delight. It's experiencing completely authentic feelings of sheer happiness when seeing a truly good thing happen to someone else. The sun shines in twofold measure as a mirror from above reflects the glow of jubilant affinity. The world could use more *firgun*. Rare. Sublime. Genuine. Joy.

So many people wake up to another day immediately feeling the weight of inadequacy pulling them down. Feeling like they don't have what it takes to make it over the next steep hill, while still feeling as though they did not do enough during some of life's toughest situations. Too often they didn't receive the acknowledgement they needed to hear. Tell someone today, if you haven't already. Remind *yourself* how you made it through, and feel the praise ring true. You did a miraculous job holding it all together in the thick of it. You've been a hero throughout it all. Yes, YOU.

LIFE'S ADVENTUROUS RIDE

Watch out for falling blessings.
Beware of frauds and hazardous facades.
Yield to oncoming heart lessons.
Stop all ways of self-sabotage.
One way to steer clear of certain danger
is do not enter a worry or gossip mind.
Give love the right-of-way, and to one another.

Slow down and enjoy life's
wild, adventurous ride.

Keep Calm and Adapt

It's been taught, and is often quite true; that the more you allow yourself to adapt, the better you are at surviving. Certain adaptation periods are, at times, confusingly uncomfortable for me. I feel like an oddly cut puzzle piece unable to honestly interlock with the entire picture, yet at the same time grateful for any tab openings when I can feel snug and relaxed. While I'm adapting, I'm not feeling entirely myself, not true to my nature, depending on the circumstance. I worry that I may be postponing my natural unfolding—or that while modifying, I may be depriving my essential features from radiantly shining through. At times, adapting feels like wearing a heavy coat that I long to shed and dance freely in the sun. These are all feelings. Eventually I'm reminded how we all come into this life immediately confronted with the necessity to acquire a variety of skills in order to conform as we evolve. In such, we become resilient over time. We progress and we thrive. While I appreciate my adaptation abilities, I rejoice when my heart can genuinely beat with complete veracity. And when the constant need to keep readjusting myself ever so intently begins fading away, the truest, most natural and prized recollections of my being surface to be honorably aligned with my surroundings. No longer feeling inured to the onslaught of unfamiliar waves that rush in to shape me, my soul can rejoice in a dance of sweet reunion.

You don't have to be so hard on yourself. You don't need to criticize the outcome of your most difficult life choices. You did what you found in yourself to do at the moment. You went to the deepest places within and came up with the best that you could provide to preserve your well-being.

Don't blame yourself or continue to bear regret for the things you had little control over.

Inside the Heart of Metamorphosis

Just when I thought I had failed to obtain what was desired of me. Just when I considered my every attempt to achieve had inevitably backfired. Every hope had fallen through; every intention, fraught with weeds. And just as I'm on the verge of being convinced these distressing moments will hollow me out completely, there I stood with empty hands while in the midst of transformation. All the while these terrible things that were making me feel quite helpless held the seeds of all that would sustain me. Yes, even in the messiness of transformation, underneath the clouded sky, something was forming deep inside like a clear and immaculate plan. My roots were fastening to each nourishing particle of soil passing by me. The sun was continuing to shine warmly within me. The water persisted to flow evenly through me—so everything I am and all I aspire to ever be, would bloom forth in its rightful time and breathe the renewing air much freely. And though you cannot see it now because it looks and feels like *ugly*; there is something achingly *beautiful* at work inside the heart of metamorphosis.

The Wisest Sage

Under the urge to become outraged, behind the impulse to be angered, and below the compulsion to satisfy your ego's immediate need to be right is a worthy gem waiting to be picked up and polished. It moves slower than any rush of reactivity. It churns sweeter and deeper than the most vehement of impatience. It is the cool and steady genius of your soul's calming wisdom—when held up to the light, will quiet the inner conflict and muffle confusion's fuss and pother. It is sharp enough to cut through the tangled resentments and layers of annoyances to expose the heart of the matter. Its reflection brings resolution as it scans the entire picture from every angle, bringing all sides into view. Yes, the wisest sage in the entire world is insightful...and all the knowledge gained illuminates profoundly within you.

Déjà Vu

I know you heard it.
You heard it in the gentle sounds
echoing a memory you thought
you lived once before.
I know you felt it.
You felt it in the rustle of
what just happened,
like a telling whisper
encoded inside a familiar kiss.
I know you've seen it.
You've already seen the delicate
shadows of what is to come,
in each stored déjà vu,
calling to you beyond the present hour.

The milky stars that aligned to announce
your birth will stay on to tell you:
Pay attention and look closely
at the significance.
Keep going this way,
for there is so much more
to come of this.

It's alright, you were not being untrue to yourself up until now. You were not living an outright lie. It was not something quick and eminently easy to recognize... that there were parts of you not ready to emerge. There were sides of you not prepared to unfold. Yet when the air became warm you did blossom. Then after the last of dry petals fell way, a subsequent existence appeared. That's how it is. So, take it all in and embrace the nature of growth and development. Allow yourself to accept what you need to expand. Acknowledge the pain it takes to produce. Despise not the form you displayed once before. You'll change from seed to a live shoot, from flower to ripe fruit— each one revealed in its own separate time. And it takes a lifespan to become what's stored inside, where dwell the many transitions to maturity.

Nestled inside your daily routine is a twofold blessing of favor and compassion, and you need not produce any evidence that you are worthy to become a recipient of life's purest forms of joy. Life merely asks this of you: Bring harm to none and surrender to the self that which wants to be expressed, then be nourished by the nectar of what allows you to fully become.

Starlit Ventures

Last night I dreamed I gathered up every daring
plan that took me outside of nowhere and threw
them out into the furthest galaxy.

As I sat back to watch the wisest of the
constellations shine, I was in awe of my
starlit ventures winking back at me.

ONLY THE HEART ROAD

I'm swept by soothing waves of gratitude washing gently through my spirit and it feels much like grace has summoned it right on time. It's best when it arrives this way and not be pressed through falsely. It's cleansing when sorrow is allowed to weep, while compassionate to loosen the grip of anger. So, when a blessing like this appears—a cut inflicted long ago, urgently tucked away as heartache, finally surfacing as clear and unexpected cries for restoration—*only the heart road is the path to take*. All other routes lead on to dead ends. And the only option is to walk in healing strides.

ART THERAPY

You didn't choose to carry it around, this box of occasional despair with bouts of dim malaise. You never wanted to drive through the thick mists of gloom—where the bright side feels more like an optimistic delusion. Even so, your heart was never far and held what was positively true: Reflections of your imagination and manifestations of your soul. And when you opened your heart, you found its desires were also there to help navigate your way out of the fog and into the clarity of artistry and expression. So, you began capturing the beauty of your surroundings. You started spreading color on a waiting canvas. You gave way to all those creative movements that would offer you comfort and healing. It has since become more than a therapeutic response to the darkness descending on your spirit. It has become your passion and strength, and the blessed mastery that allows you to steer away from the haziness of disconnect, but merge instead with the brilliant and fascinating inner sense of vitality contained within. Your art calms you now. Your pictures display inward joy. And when you're at one with your craft, it's like swimming in warm, peaceful waters.

Our voyage to the truth is an inside trek where our wounded and broken hearts can be transfigured to a more beautiful and spiritual state of being.

And therein lies your real healing...

ACCEPTANCE

A certain acceptance began while I didn't know how long it would take to get to *much later.* It continued on when I wasn't sure how much time *only for a while* could last. I wasn't aware of the days or where I was going, or the presence of any definitive closure—not even the thickening skin that had formed a tender scar to bind a raw and opened gash. At one time in my mind's eye was preserved a vivid image, yet would eventually pale. I watched the warm glow of the moon diffuse the darkness of night, then vanish inside each faint and passing hour. A malleable memory gradually becomes a sheer and delicate body slipping away and out of my hands and into the air. That's how this acceptance began. Not like the closing chapter of a cherished book, or the sweet sadness of a wilting flower. It was not like a peaceful cloth meant for clutching desperately close to a grievously seeping part of my heart, no. But more like a last call to remembrance. It was surely there, but got lost somewhere inside of a bell's chime in the wind; clamorously resounding at first, then ethereally haunting before fading still.

I know that of all the pains you hold inside, the sadness emanating from a great loss can feel the heaviest, at times leaving your soul gasping for air. Sometimes you'll allow the sorrow to lead you as far back as you can go just to squeeze that familiar place into your chest, once again. Maybe they will never entirely vanish, all the many ways of missing. Yet by some means, when you unveiled the utter tenderness of your grief to be exposed before all of life remaining, you softened into such a genuine and vulnerable space. You revealed a million precious tears stored within an immense and giving heart. And although mourning does not seem to completely disappear, that heart continues in its pulse, living boldly in beauty— and with time, still offering an open field to meet with true connections and greet the many forms of love.

THE GIFT OF COMPASSION

Your wound is not meant to become a cloak of silent misery. It was stifled for many years and can speak freely now, for there can be no understanding of pain if it is ignored. And there is little space for love to flow freely when the anguish of past harm has not been considered and acknowledged. There was a time when I always felt merciful and caring for others but the most important component was not present: self-compassion. I was not able to recognize my suppressed emotions, although later I gently accepted that I was not being self-loving because I did all that I knew to do. But when I finally allowed the hushed hurt to emerge, fully travailing, it was like a sudden birth of the purest form of loving kindness. This new tenderness reached back again and further inward to comfort the other forgotten remnants and brokenness within myself. This is the nature of compassion. And now I can love myself fully, maintaining the balance between self and others. I could read about it and I could ask, but until I experienced it for myself, there was no way to hold the profound appreciation for such compassion. Compassion is the gift that deepens our human understanding.

Everything

We use the word everything to express anything of
utmost importance.
*She was my everything. It took me everything I had.
I gave him everything. Everything I am...*
Everything is the entire situation.
Everything is what matters.
Everything is sacred.

With all that said, still I find I can't adequately explain
the concept of everything to someone who has never
made a decision or taken any action in the name of love
and courage that entails the risk of losing it all entirely.

Life will take you to some unexpected places.
Use caution, check both ways.
Proceed with passion...

What are you wearing? A customized stigma you didn't ask for? Negative generalizations patterned by society? Maybe a few personal opinions tailored to fit all your misconceptions...

Take them off. Take them all off. All the false stories, the ill-fitting notions, and any lingering judgements unfairly pinned to your character. If it must be continually adjusted, if it looks and feels somehow wrong, if it's too restrictive or much too loose, you need not wear it. It doesn't fit. *It's not you.* It doesn't belong.

THANK YOU, YEAR

I wanted to blame you. I wanted to make you responsible for every death and negative outcome, and for all the complicated obstacles set in my way. I wanted to shake my fist at your delivering grief to my door and turn my back on the sorrow you dealt. I wanted to desensitize my heart in the middle of your tragedy and misfortune, and numb myself from the onslaught of fear engulfing me throughout your cataclysm. Instead, I will stand in the place that's called gratitude and I will say, *thank you*. Thank you, world, for holding me in your grace each night. Thank you, life, for keeping me in your protective care. Thank you, friends, for walking with me in the dark, because I made it through to see the light of the next passage. Thank you, hardship, for bringing out the real work that needed to be done from within to allow for growth and transition. And the vital truth is, whatever we so love is divinely passing through. Every living thing, every precious soul, every single moment—every leaf on the wind—will not ever be repeated. So, on this last given day when one final road renders itself to one new, I will say," *Thank you, year, for bringing me here"*.

A single vibrant soul can stir all the colors into life
where one hundred vital forces could not go.

THE MAPS WITHIN MY TEARS

Philosophy arrived in time
to rationalize my fears,
while all of reason could not find
the maps within my tears.
And the logic of my mind
could not make sense
of what my heart
had engineered—
But wisdom knows each
drop I cried
charts a world
I hold so dear.

Reliving the sharp edges of an unburied hatchet. Pacing up and down the corridor of unpleasant bygones. Resentment has an underhanded way of allowing past offenses to barge in and steal the light of your present. Yes, you were injured at one time by another's actions, but they have no power to hold you in everlasting bondage after you've worked to be free of those chains. Look compassionately within yourself to bring healing to your own wounds and not become a servant to another's wrongdoing. Forgive yourself and release the haunting pain. Now begin to live in the freshness of presence and self-honor.

Speaking Out After an Assault

There comes a time when the dark shadows of guilt and shame, fear and blame, and stigma's stain can no longer hold the purest light as captive. There comes a time when scorn and judgment cease to be the diligent wardens of an imprisoned story. And there comes a time when a trauma inflicted and subsequently buried is resurrected, its cries heard and recognized as the emerging steps towards healing. An assault does not abruptly end after the initial attack, but tragically leaves the survivor with an aftermath of emotional responses that may activate fear, even years later. In a culture swimming in triggering material, it has been a positive thing for more and more women to come together to reveal their painful experiences as true lights of grace and dignity, making the reality of rape and assault impossible to ignore. No longer hostages of secret trauma, abuse or violation, they have been supportively received and acknowledged. We must stand with our sisters and daughters as shining lights of truth who have proclaimed their freedom by speaking out and have courageously taken the heart road to recovery. Our only option now is that we continue, upholding all that is right with heads held high, and to walk in healing strides.

BLUEPRINTS

Listening to each other's stories, connecting and engaging, witnessing one another. These are the ways we discover the blueprints of our own great plan, how we map out a clearer sense of meaning and purpose, and how we can locate and identify exactly where we store our deep wisdom. We share the same valuable time, space and worth to relate and experience kinship and inclusion, and altogether reflect our divine being.

Not everything happens for a good or cosmic reason. Not everything has been orchestrated by otherworldly forces to present a life lesson. Why bad things happen to the innocent is a mystery that will never be unraveled. Thankfully there is no mystery in the wonderment of healing. And by picking up the mortar and pestle that are the emotional healing tools, we can be the alchemist that takes charge, remarkably exchanging the seemingly irreversible energy within the violations against us for the precious elements of restoration. As we place them into the crucible to be processed and exchanged for indisputable strength and with a more supportive and affirming existence, we overcome and create real meaning. We come into our wholeness as a triumphant human being.

LETTING GO OF FEAR

I'm not ashamed to admit I carried a mixed bag of fear for certain things throughout my life. Recoiling in absolute fright, at times. Fright anxiously pushing at my insides in the rush of every day. Tremendously disliking the confusion my fear wrought and the frazzle of dismay. But now I no longer resent fear since deliberately refraining from trying to overcome it with a fighting warrior posture. Instead, I began to attentively listen to her deep-rooted apprehensions. She had so much to tell me, so much anxiousness that would only be calmed by a sure presence of reassurance and faith. She wanted to be met with love and allowed an explanation, then be offered an opening to be liberated. No longer a ball of fire in denial, over time an authentic bravery emerged. From out of qualm came steady confidence when met face-to-face with those dreadful things that had disquieted me once before. And it was inside the many grounding lessons where these daunting misgivings found a way out that I discovered a veracious daring within, its heart beating like a dauntless, spirited lion.

The child you love, the child you think you know, could be gay and scared. The child you raised to be respectful to others might be longing to transform gender, yet frightened to the core because other transgender people were bullied, hurt or murdered. The children we care deeply about, who are too afraid to be open and come out, can begin to live in the truth of their essence when we actively care about protecting their civil right to live in safety. To provide our children with the emotional freedom to make these life choices is imperative to creating a peaceful world. Adults and parents, unite to thoroughly shift the mindset of society to embrace everyone for who they are as a human being. Become caring examples of love and acceptance by being allied and supportive of the LGBTQ community.

Gratitude speaks every language, has crossed
every boundary, and traversed every sea.

One day you'll know it. Maybe it will be as you're standing in a lush meadow or an intuitive green forest and you become tender to the artistry of nature and receptive to the stark reality of its beauty. And then you will feel it. Somehow, you'll perceive all the natural wonder and its promise to be present and true. You become comfortable with yourself, suddenly, along with the trees and the songbirds and the miniscule animals who thrive within the balance and intricacy of each scattered moss bed. You can sense this secluded world holds no expectation, but feel the soft insistence that you're a part of this family, and lean into its coaxing to allow yourself to belong. Then as you're opening to the calming breeze landing faintly against your cheek, you contemplate the clear motion of air delicately sweeping across the wings of that one passing butterfly. Its fleeting life is sure, yet in the slightest flutter there whispers to you such great and lasting offerings. *To transfer this existing beauty into your very heart; to dive further into yourself; to give in to your innermost joy. And find healing.*

You will not be forgotten. In the flurry of this season brightly lit with cheerful songs and festive parties, you are not alone nor have you slipped out of sight, invisible or unknown. Recalled are the many ways you kept it in mind to help others without asking for anything in return or expecting praise. Recognized are the countless times you remained aware of someone else in need and genuinely cared. You've a heart of precious gold. And because you remembered, you will not ever be forgotten.

Worn Surfaces

I love worn surfaces and stains.
I love ridges and creases,
and textures with wise grains.
I love the rustic feel
of a woven textile,
or a tabletop blemished
with deep furrows and lines.
I love faces that show
they've been here,
with hearts that hold experiences
and memories of a lifetime.
I love scars that were scratches,
and tea spills, and knotted pines...
I love those wrinkles
beside your eyes
that draw me to your smile.

Lionhearted

I've grown to admire the risk taker who stands willing to make daring ventures, knowing full well the possibility of being broken open, yet undeterred and feels it far better to try than not. I reverently give thanks to the valiant one who perseveres in their journey, defying any oppression or infirmity set before them, soldiering on with unheard of determination. But it was the lionhearted, ultimately, that I came to be in of absolute awe. The relentless fighter biting right through life challenges, despite all their doubts and regardless of the endless list of fears and personal struggles. They don't understand the meaning of the word *quit*, courageously focused, knowing nothing ever comes with ease. You can see it in their stance, hear it in their spirit's roar, feel it in their regal presence, because such stalwart fearlessness cannot easily hide. They're never giving up on dreams. Never holding to past regrets. They are a noble lion with a warrior's heart, beating ferociously alive.

Homecoming

We are driven to find ourselves, although some use this energy to evade the process altogether. But for the one who seeks waits the most wonderful of homecomings. Each time you make an imperceptible or the most striking new discovery. Each opportunity you elect to open the closet of hidden secrets. And any chance you take to unravel a wildly tangled inner mystery, you become reunited with your true self, where the indwelling of love resides. You, the beloved.

You Belong

You are a soul
and you have a right to shine
in all those places
you long to venture.

To be witnessed,
to be heard,
to confess
and be seen.
You belong.

Carve out your shining moon
and place it high among the stars
to gleam forever.

You've been through some of the darkest reaches in life; often believing that the coming out from them has made you more inept than the going in. As you question your choices, doubt has been the shadow companion cast beside those struggling steps just to make it. Take heart weary one, you walk a noble path. You're treading within the divinity of what you are becoming, where in the face of uncertainty your authentic heart and sense of deep purpose reflect the light of your higher self. It takes some time to figure things out...and you will get there in time.

ACKNOWLEDGMENTS

My deep gratitude to the many people who have joined me on social media to offer me support. You are the stars in the sky I look up to. My wholehearted thanks to Allyson Woodrooffe, whose artistry, skill, and creative brilliance have made this book beautiful. Clara Macri, Kelly McNelis, David Sandum, Ivan M. Granger, Dean Pasch, Chris Saade, Jayananda...thank you for being there for me. Lindsay Taylor, my heart with limbs, my laughter, the light of my life. Thank you for being my daughter and inspiring some of these passages. My thanks to Barbara Boruff and John Frybort, for their unconditional love and affirming wisdom. Robert, thank you for being with me in spirit. And Sophie cat, thank you for listening close as I read you these passages, never once meowing unfavorably.

Above all, I want to thank the love of my life, my husband Jeffrey, for his unwavering support while we put this book together, even in the late hours; for his belief in my passion for poetry and written expression; for his fierce love and for his everlasting encouragement to pursue my dreams.

About The Author

Susan Frybort is an American-born poet with a deep fascination for life and the human experience. Writing since she was a child, her poems and affirmations are a tapestry of wisdom and compassion that soften the heart's edges, calling us home. Previously published in *Elephant Journal*, *Vivid Life*, and *Women for One*, she has published two inspiring books. Her first, the poetry collection *Hope is a Traveler*, was published in 2015 to rave reviews. 'Hope' engages the senses through imagery and metaphor. Her second book, *Open Passages*, is a special collection of meditations and affirmations that offer soothing balm to the weary soul. Susan is also a skilled tailor and a soft-spoken comedienne. She enjoys rescuing Balinese kittens, eating Vietnamese Pho, watching disaster films, and listening to Arvo Pärt. She is a proud mother to her brilliant daughter, Lindsay. Susan currently lives in Canada with her husband, author Jeff Brown.